FIFTY YEARS SINCE THE END OF STEAM

BRITAIN'S RAILWAYS 1968–2018

MARK LEE INMAN

AMBERLEY

To Pud and Gillie - two wonderful girls!

First published 2018

Amberley Publishing
The Hill, Stroud,
Gloucestershire, GL5 4EP

www.amberley-books.com

ISBN: 978 1 4456 7674 6 (print)
ISBN: 978 1 4456 7675 3 (ebook)

British Library Cataloguing in Publication Data.
A catalogue record for this book is available from the British Library.

Typeset in 10pt on 13pt Celeste.
Origination by Amberley Publishing.
Printed in the UK.

Contents

Introduction

Britain's railways finished with steam in 1968, but it was not the beginning of a golden era. The last fifty years have seen periods of neglect and underinvestment, political meddling and frequent reorganisations. Only in the post-privatisation era has there been a serious commitment by operators and government to major investment. Even now, there remains a substantial backlog.

This is a photographic chronology of these years. It is not exhaustive, but the colour photographs do capture the numerous changes and accompanying livery changes. Cynical observers could be forgiven for declaring that the only beneficiaries were the paint makers.

The 1970s was an era of corporate monotony. There was little to cheer about. The electrification from London to Glasgow, promised in the 1955 Modernisation Plan, was eventually completed in 1974. It would be the 1990s before the East Coast and the Great Eastern main lines beyond Colchester would be electrified. The branch line to Felixstowe, now serving one of Britain's busiest container ports, remains a single track branch line devoid of electrification.

The greatest success of the 1970s was the introduction of the 125 mph High Speed Train – a diesel service initially operating from London Paddington, Bristol and Cardiff on the former Great Western Main Line, which brought a new standard of speed and comfort on these key services. Further batches of these trains later entered service on the East Coast Main Line.

The 1980s saw sectorisation – the creation of InterCity as a separate entity, provincial services being hived off, and serious progress on the fulfilment of a promise in the Transport Act of 1968 – as well as better trains and services for the regional conurbations through the local Passenger Transport Executives.

Scotland's railways were hived off as a separate entity – ScotRail, which, through a combination of good management and government commitment, has proved extremely successful.

Another success story of the late 1980s was Network SouthEast, where all the passenger services running into London were placed under one organisational umbrella.

Freight operations were broken up into different product-related activities. Part of the Beeching philosophy had been to encourage the railways to do what they did best – bulk haulage and containers, hence Freightliner. Open access was to lead to freight operations that were destined to go through further changes.

The change in technology led to many of the more successful diesel locomotives being built by experienced private contractors. In turn, the rundown of railway workshops has led to less train building in the United Kingdom, and trains being bought in from overseas builders.

The 1990s brought the era of privatisation. Driven by political doctrine and an obsession with public sector borrowing, the railways were broken into franchises, the geographic area frequently matching the territories of the old 1923 Grouping with the return of the Great Eastern, the London & South Western and the South Eastern.

At best, privatisation has been a curate's egg. The railways are not free from political meddling. Many franchise contracts have been too short to allow meaningful strategic planning and there appears to be no reward for good operating.

Even so, passengers on the Great Eastern from Liverpool Street to Shenfield enjoy an unprecedented high-frequency service, which is due to be enhanced still further by Crossrail or the Elizabeth Line. Elsewhere there has been considerable investment in new rolling stock. However, some of the franchises have proved less than successful, with the East Coast being taken back into temporary state ownership. Likewise, the operation of the track and signalling has been taken back into public ownership. Elsewhere, other achievements have been marred by a deterioration in labour relations. While in part this is due to trade union bloody-mindedness, the real blame has to be placed unequivocally at the door of arrogant, remote and questionably competent politicians and management.

Even so, there is the prospect of more new trains and better services. Rail travel has seen unprecedented growth in the last twenty years. Since 2000, fifteen lines, closed or mothballed by Beeching, have been reopened, as have stations. There is the real prospect of further rejuvenation, especially where communities are expanding as the population grows. Open access passenger services have successfully connected provincial cities such as Bradford and Hartlepool directly to the capital. Similarly, the freight business has expanded, although the growth in container traffic has to be countered with the loss of heavy bulk freight, such as coal. Although cuts have been made in the original plans and promises, the Great Western Main Line is in the process of being electrified to Bristol and Cardiff. It is possible that the former Midland Main Line from London St Pancras to Sheffield may eventually get the same long-awaited treatment, likewise the trans-Pennine services, and the Great Eastern line to Norwich is to get new trains. This book attempts to portray these changes.

While I annotated the photographs at the time as best I could, I have had to undertake a certain amount of research. Brian Morrison's *British Rail DMUs and Diesel Railcars* has proved invaluable. For local history, J. E. Connor's *Liverpool Street to Ilford* and Mitchell and Smith's *North London Line* have been equally helpful. Various railway websites have also been invaluable. A few photographs have had to be brought in, and I hope I have correctly ascribed them. I sincerely apologise if I have erred where they are concerned.

For the technical, in the early days, the trustworthy and reliable Voigtländer was the camera used. Early in the 1980s I graduated to SLR with an Olympus, which has since been replaced by a Canon digital camera. In the days of roll film both Kodak and Agfa were used, with increased ASA value.

As always, I have to thank my long-suffering wife, who concedes that these exercises keep me out of mischief. The encouragement and support of Connor Stait and the team at Amberley must also be acknowledged.

The 1970s – The Blue Era

To Begin at the Beginning...

It is 10.30 a.m. on a warm summer morning in June 1968. In the best tradition, the Cornish Rivera leaves Paddington for Penzance behind a brace of Class 42 'Warship' diesel-hydraulic locomotives.

The Western Region of British Railways preferred diesel-hydraulic locomotives. The German V200 was a proven design and the Warships were built at Swindon and by the North British Locomotive works under license.

Class 42 Warship D804 *Avenger*

D804 *Avenger* entered traffic in April 1959. Although steam still had two months left to live, the decision had been taken to dispense with non-standard forms of traction, and *Avenger* and her partner were already on death row. The locomotive was withdrawn and scrapped in March 1972. Two locomotives survive in preservation.

Class 35 B-B Hymeks

Introduced in 1961 and dubbed 'Hymeks' because of their Mekydro hydraulic transmission, they were mixed-traffic locomotives for secondary passenger workings and local freight. Early in their career, many were roistered onto the Paddington–South Wales express services with indifferent success. Under the 1967/68 National Traction Plan they were deemed non-standard and withdrawal commenced in 1971, which was completed by 1974. Four are preserved.

Class 52 C-C Westerns

The Class 52 Westerns were introduced in 1961 to provide a more powerful locomotive on Paddington to West of England and South Wales services. Prior to the imposition of the corporate blue, many appeared in different colours, with maroon, green and even desert sand and golden ochre appearing. Naming the class was a nice touch, with 'Western' preceding some military or heraldic noun. Again, poor reliability and the National Traction Plan meant that withdrawal began in 1970 and was completed in 1979. Seven survived into preservation.

Seen here is D1010 *Western Campaigner*. Built in 1962, she was withdrawn and passed into preservation and the care of the Diesel & Electric Preservation Group. During the period 1987/89, she masqueraded as *Western Yeoman*, and it is in this green-liveried guise that she is seen at Didcot in May 1987.

Class 08 No. 08495, 0-6-0 Diesel-Electric Shunter, 350 hp

Based on an earlier LMS design, these locomotives were built over the period of 1952 to 1962. In total, 996 locomotives were built, making it one of the most numerous locomotive classes. They were a familiar sight around stations and marshalling yards. Changes in railway operations gradually rendered many of them redundant, with many being stored, scrapped or even sold. Around 100 are still in service with various railway operators, with a further seventy on preserved railways. Built at Doncaster in 1958, No. 08495 worked at Stratford, but from 1976 it spent periods of time in store. Captured at Hitchin in 1987, it has survived into preservation on the North Yorkshire Moors Railway.

Class 20 No. 20169, Bo-Bo, 1,000 hp

A total of 228 of this highly successful and reliable design were built by English Electric between 1957 and 1968. They usually served as freight locomotives, typically going around in pairs. Withdrawal started in the 1990s, but twenty-two are still active on the main line, while a further twenty-two survive in preservation. No. 20169 forms the leader of the pair on an enthusiast special run along the Redmire branch in North Yorkshire in September 1992. It had entered service in 1957 and was withdrawn in December 2001.

Class 26 No. 26039, Bo-Bo, 1,160 hp

The Class 26 was a medium-powered mixed-traffic locomotive that was built in 1958–59 and initially allocated to the London area. Following successful evaluation in Scotland, the whole class was allocated to Scotland and employed on a wide variety of duties. Routine withdrawal began in 1977, with the last members of the class being finally withdrawn in 1993. No. 26039 entered traffic in September 1959 and is captured at Carlisle in April 1988 sporting the Eastfield (Glasgow) 'Scotty Dog' motif.

Class 27 No. 27059 (Nos 27205, 27123), Bo-Bo, 1,250 hp

A development of the earlier Class 26, sixty-nine Class 27 locomotives were built in 1961–62, and by 1969 the entire class was operating in Scotland. For many years they were extensively used on the West Highland Line to Oban and Fort William and the demanding 90 mph shuttle service between Edinburgh and Glasgow until being replaced by Class 47s in 1980. New in 1962, No. 27039 was one of the locomotives used on the Edinburgh–Glasgow shuttle service. Withdrawn in July 1987, it was purchased by the Severn Valley Railway and turned out in pristine condition complete with large Eastfield 'Scotty Dog' at the Basingstoke open day in September 1987.

Class 31 No. 31451, A1A-A1A, 1,250 to 1,470 hp

Another of the early pilot scheme successes, 263 Class 31 locomotives were built by Brush from 1957 to 1962. Subject to many modifications, they spent much of their working lives on the former Eastern Region and particularly in East Anglia. No. 31451 had entered service as D5852 in August 1962. It was fitted with electric train heating and renumbered 31451. Showing how bland and uninteresting the Beeching blue could be, the locomotive is seen on pilot duty at King's Cross in May 1987. It was withdrawn in March 1996 and scrapped in September 1998 after over thirty-three years of service.

Class 33/2 Crompton No. 33203, Bo-Bo

The Class 33 was built between 1960 and 1962 for the non-electrified sections of the former Southern Region. The nickname derived from their Crompton Parkinson electrical transmission. The twelve members of subclass 33/2 were equipped with narrow bodies for the Hastings line and earned the sobriquet 'Slim Jims'. No. 33203 was delivered in 1960, and it is seen at Waterloo in July 1987. It was withdrawn in March 1991.

English Electric, Class 37, Co-Co

One of the real success stories of the Modernisation Plan, 309 Class 37s were built by English Electric between 1960 and 1965. Possessing a wide range of route availability, they could be seen in almost any part of the country, from East Anglia to the Scottish Highlands, on almost every kind of duty. Sporting the corporate blue livery, this unidentified example brings an Up excursion from Clacton through Shenfield, Essex, on a summer Sunday evening in the late 1970s.

Class 45 Peaks No. 45114, 1Co-Co1, 2,500 hp

Built by British Railways at Crewe and Derby, they operated on the Midland Main Line until 1982, and later the trans-Pennine services from Liverpool to Leeds, York and Newcastle. Others could be seen on the North East to South West cross-country services. They were progressively withdrawn during the 1980s, with the last being withdrawn in 1989. No. 45114 was built at Crewe in April 1961. It seen at York on a cross-country service in July 1986. The locomotive was withdrawn in 1987.

Class 47 No. 47489, Co-Co, 2,580 hp (Initially 2,750 hp)

Developed by Brush, 512 Class 47 locomotives were built between 1962 and 1968 as part of the steam replacement programme. A familiar sight all over the country, a measure of the design's success is that eighty-one still exist as of October 2016, with thirty still operational. A further thirty have been rebuilt into Class 57 and also remain operational. No. 47489 entered traffic in February 1964 and is seen powering a northbound express through Barnt Green towards Birmingham in the summer of 1990. It was withdrawn and scrapped in October 2007 after forty-three years of service.

Class 50 No. 50037 *Illustrious*, Co-Co, 2,700 hp

Built by English Electric at the Vulcan Foundry in 1967–68, the Class 50 locomotives were initially leased to British Railways. They initially operated on the then still un-electrified West Coast Main Line from Preston to Glasgow. This enabled the schedule of the prestigious Royal Scot service to be accelerated to six hours by the early 1970s – the same as the pre-war steam-hauled Coronation Scot. After completion of the electrification to Glasgow, the locomotives were transferred to the Western Region to replace the remaining unreliable diesel-hydraulics. At the time, the whole class received names commemorating famous warships. Replaced by the HSTs, they were confined to West of England services out of London Waterloo. Final withdrawals were in 1994.

No. 50037 was delivered into service in September 1968. It is seen sporting the revised British Railways largo logo corporate blue at Old Oak Common in September 1985. Sister locomotive No. 50031 *Hood*, also sporting the large logo, can be glimpsed in the right background.

Class 55 Deltic No. 55014 *Duke of Wellington's Regiment*, Co-Co, 3,300 hp

Heralded as the world's most powerful single-unit diesel, twenty-two Class 55 locomotives were built to replace the Gresley Pacifics on the East Coast Main Line from London to Edinburgh where they dominated the top link services until the advent of the HSTs in 1978. From 1978 to 1981 they were relegated to semi-fast or parcels services with withdrawal taking place during 1980–81. No. 55014 was new in September 1961 and is seen waiting to leave King's Cross on a semi fast working to York in December 1980. The locomotive was withdrawn in November 1981.

Class 56 No. 56112, Co-Co, 3,250 hp

A large class of 135 locomotives designed for heavy freight work introduced in 1976, the first thirty Class 56 locomotives were built in Romania. The mesh-like cover over the horns earned the locomotives the sobriquet 'Grids'. High maintenance needs, high operating costs and availability issues led to early withdrawal. A large number were taken out of service in 2004. No. 56112 sports the large logo blue livery as she hauls a northbound coal working through Newcastle-upon-Tyne in the summer of 1987. She was withdrawn in 2003.

Class 73 No. 73104, Electro-Diesel, 1,420 hp/600 hp

Forty years before SNCF introduced their dual-mode multiple units, British Railways Southern Region introduced a 650/750 volt DC third-rail electric locomotive equipped with a 600 hp diesel for use on non-electrified lines. Forty-three were built at English Electric's Vulcan Foundry from 1967 to 1968, and twenty-seven remain active with various rail operators. No. 73104 entered service in July 1967 and is seen outside London Waterloo sporting the large logo livery in November 1986. It is still operational.

Class 81 No. 81019, Bo-Bo, 25 kV Electric, 3,388 hp

A batch of twenty-five locomotives built for use on all services out of Euston along the West Coast Main Line, the Class 81s were later relegated to secondary duties, such as station pilot and ECS workings, and were withdrawn in the 1990s. No. 81019 entered traffic in September 1961. Sporting the Glasgow Shields leaping salmon motif, it is seen at Euston in July 1987, having been substituted on an Anglo-Scottish working. The locomotive was withdrawn in 1989.

Class 85 No. 85011, Bo-Bo, 3,200 hp

A class of forty Class 85 locos were built between 1961 and 1964 for the West Coast electrification. No. 85011 entered traffic in April 1962 and is seen at Euston in the late 1980s. It was withdrawn in 1991.

Class 86 No. 86237 *Sir Charles Halle*, Bo-Bo, 3,600 hp

The Class 86 is one of the star success stories of the Modernisation Plan. A total of 100 were built between 1965 and 1966 to work the West Coast Main Line. In the early 1980s, several, including No. 86237, were reallocated to the Great Eastern route to Norwich. Others were modified to become purely freight locomotives. Some have even been exported to work in Eastern Europe, while fourteen remain in service with Freightliner.

No. 86237 *Sir Charles Halle* entered into traffic December 1965. Its name reflects the link with places and people associated with the West Coast route. Following the completion of the electrification to Norwich, the locomotive was aptly renamed the *University of East Anglia*. Seen at London Euston in October 1986, the locomotive was eventually withdrawn in 2004 after over thirty-eight years of service.

Multiple Units – Diesel Mechanical Multiple Units

British Rail corporate identity initially had the blue/grey for main line and InterCity passenger rolling stock, and an all-over blue for stock engaged on local, commuter and branch line work.

The rather drab all-over blue did not last long and the blue/grey combination gradually spread to all categories of passenger rolling stock.

Class 104 No. M53479

A total of 300 Class 104 vehicles were built for general branch line and local services by the Birmingham Railway Carriage & Wagon Company from April 1957. Many survived in service until the 1990s. With No. M53479 leading, and still sporting the all-over blue livery, a Class 104 unit pauses at Walthamstow (Blackhorse Road) on a Barking to Gospel Oak service in April 1987.

Class 107 No. 107743

Built at BR Derby works for Scottish Region local services between December 1960 and June 1961, the class members were initially turned out in corporate overall blue. They were repainted first in blue/grey, before many received the distinctive Strathclyde PTE orange/black livery. The last members of the class survived until 1991/92. No. 107743 stands at the buffers in Glasgow (Central) station late on a summer's evening in 1987.

Class 116 No. M53902

Built at BR Derby in April 1957 for suburban duties, the units worked in the Birmingham area and in South Wales. Refurbished during the 1970s, many units survived into the mid-1990s. With No. M53902 nearest the camera, a Tyesley-based Class 116 unit rests over at Machynlleth (Ceridigion) in July 1987.

Class 119 No. 119590

The Modernisation Plan recognised the need for a multiple unit capable of operating cross-country services with a reasonable degree of comfort and facilities. As a result, the Class 119 contained a buffet facility and was gangwayed throughout. Built in October 1958, withdrawals began in the late 1980s, with the final withdrawal taking place in 1995. No. 119590 brings up the rear of a service from West Wales into Swansea as it descends the Landore curve on its final approach to Swansea (High Street) station in July 1987.

Class 202 No. 202001

Ostensibly, this is one of the second batch of units. No. 202001 is seen at Hastings on a special shuttle working between Ashford and Hastings working for 'NetWork Day' in November 1987.

The Southern Region's (SR) choice for electric transmission for its diesel-electric multiple units (DEMUs) was based upon capitalising on existing skills in the intricacies of electric traction, the employment of a tried and tested English Electric power unit, and traction motors that were common to existing electric multiple units (EMUs).

The initial Class 201 was built at the SR Eastleigh Works in May 1957 to work between London Charing Cross and Hastings. The Class 202 followed later in the year. The units survived, giving reliable service until the Hastings line was electrified in 1986. Several carriages and power units have passed into preservation.

Electric Multiple Units 25 kV Overhead
The Great Eastern Railway out of London's Liverpool Street station had considered electrification in the early years of the twentieth century as a way of coping with increasingly heavy commuter traffic. After the First World War, the LNER eventually announced an electrification scheme using 1,500 volts DC from Liverpool Street to Shenfield in 1935. Delayed by the Second World War, the electric service eventually started in 1949, and was converted to the 25 kV AC system in November 1960.

Class 307 No. 307119

Built at Eastleigh between 1954 and 1956, initially as 1,500 volt DC units, the Class 307s were converted to 25 kV AC in 1960. Refurbished in the mid-1980s, these units were withdrawn in 1991, although several were overhauled and repainted to work the electrified sections of the West Yorkshire Metro PTE. Driving trailers were converted for use with postal services. No. 307119 arrives at Romford on a working to Southend (Victoria) in March 1987.

Class 302 No. 302203

Introduced from 1958 to 1960, some units were allocated to work the newly electrified London, Tilbury & Southend (LTS) line out of Fenchurch Street. Withdrawn in 1999, some of the vehicles were used as driving trailers for parcel workings. No. 302203 is seen on an Up working passing through Stratford in August 1987. A Network SouthEast branding sticker can be seen on the side of the leading driving trailer.

Class 304 No. 304040

Built for suburban work primarily around Liverpool, Crewe and Manchester, the introduction of the sloping front to the cab marked a big improvement over the earlier rather bland designs. All were withdrawn by 1996. No. 304040 is seen at Crewe in July 1987.

Class 310 No. 310053

Further design and style improvements can be seen in the Class 310 introduced in 1963. Designed to work suburban services out of London Euston and Birmingham as part of the West Coast electrification, the units were eventually cascaded to the LTS and were finally withdrawn in 2002, having done almost forty years of service. No. 310053 is seen arriving at London Euston in August 1987.

Class 312 No. 312704

Introduced in 1975, these units were to be the last slam-door units. Initially used on the Great Northern King's Cross to Royston services, with a few being retained to work around Birmingham, they were cascaded to the Great Eastern and the London, Tilbury & Southend lines in the early 1980 where they were warmly welcomed. Eventually, these units fell victim to the trend away from slam-door stock and were finally withdrawn in 2003. No. 312704 is captured racing through Harold Wood (Essex) on an Up working in November 1986.

Above and below: Class 313, 25 kV AC/750 Volt DC (Third Rail)

A dual-voltage unit built at York in 1967–77, these units were the first of the second generation EMUs and the first dual-voltage units. Initially designed for the Great Northern inner suburban services running over former London Tube lines from London Moorgate to Welwyn Garden City and Hertford, some served on the North London line, West London lines and the Watford DC lines out of Euston until they were eventually replaced in 2010 by the new Class 378 units. In DC mode, No. 313017 (*above*) leaves Dalston (Kingsland) and will follow the DC lines to Islington and Willesden Junction in July 1987, while in AC mode, No. 313031 (*below*) approaches Finsbury Park en route for Moorgate, also in July 1987.

Class 314 No. 314208

Built in 1979 for the inner suburban services of the Strathclyde PTE, and still in service, the Class 314s are now the oldest EMUs operating for Strathclyde. With the introduction of the Class 380 and 385 units, it is likely they will be withdrawn in the near future. No. 314208 sports the striking Strathclyde orange/black livery, and proudly proclaims 'Strathclyde Transport' as it pauses at Finnieston en route to Dalmuir in August 1990.

Electric Multiple Units 660–750 Volts DC (Third Rail)

Much of the former Southern Railway had already been electrified under this system when the railways were nationalised in 1948.

Class 416/3 (2EPB) No. 6321

It was policy to build two-car units to supplement services during the rush hour. Intended for inner suburban services, and built from 1951 to 1961, they too survived into the 1990s, having gone through a refurbishment programme in the early 1980s. One of the refurbished units, No. 6321, was deployed in 1985 to work on the North London line and is depicted at Highbury & Islington station on a working to Richmond in April 1987.

Class 438 (4TC) No. 8034

The Class 4TC (Trailer Control) were non-powered three- and four-car units converted from locomotive-hauled carriages during 1967–8 and 1974. This was a cost effective (?) solution to the problem of providing a service to Weymouth after the end of Southern steam in 1967, when electrification through to Weymouth could not be justified. One or two such units would be propelled by a 3,200 hp 4REP (Restaurant Electro-Pneumatic) unit from Waterloo to Bournemouth. At Bournemouth, one or two units would be detached and hauled forward to Weymouth by a Class 33/1 locomotive. On the return run, the units were propelled back to Bournemouth by the locomotive. The units were rendered surplus when the line to Weymouth was eventually electrified in 1988 and the units were withdrawn by 1991. No. 8034 is seen at London Waterloo in April 1987.

The Rise of the Passenger Transport Executive (PTE)

Barbara Castle's Transport Act of 1968 created the PTEs to provide coordination of public transport in the major conurbations of England and Scotland. The first five, covering Birmingham, Glasgow, Liverpool, Manchester and Tyneside, came into being between 1969 and 1973. As a result of the Local Government Act of 1972, the existing PTE boundaries were made coterminous with the new counties and two PTEs were created for West and South Yorkshire. With the creation of the Strathclyde region in Scotland, the Greater Glasgow PTE was extended to cover the whole region.

In the early years, the PTEs had to make do with what they inherited. We will follow their fortunes and progress through the decades.

Strathclyde, Class 303 No. 303204

Strathclyde was a little more fortunate than some others. The celebrated state-of-the-art 'Blue Train' electrics had been introduced in 1960 for the North Clyde electrification. Constructed by Pressed Steel at Linwood in Renfrewshire, they featured stylish wrap-round windows and pneumatically operated sliding passenger doors. They survived until December 2002. Refurbished No. 303024 sports the striking Strathclyde orange/black livery at Glasgow Central in August 1988.

Merseyrail, Class 507 No. 507121

Electrification came early to Liverpool's suburban lines. The LMS had inherited a third-rail system from the Lancashire & Yorkshire Railway. The Class 507s, from the same family as the Classes 313–318, replaced the LMS units. Over the years, the system has also been extended. No. 507121 still sports the blue/grey with a Merseyrail sticker as it arrives at Birkenhead en route for New Brighton in April 1989.

Two Jewels in the Crown

Two shining success stories from the 1970s are the final completion of the West Coast electrification in 1974, nineteen years after it had been promised in the 1955 Modernisation Plan, and the High Speed Train (HST).

Class 87 No. 87012 *Couer-de-Lion*, Bo-Bo, 5,000 hp

On the completion of West Coast electrification, thirty-six locomotives were built in 1974. The increased power was to provide for greater speed and to cope with the demands of the route north of Crewe. They remained the mainstay of the West Coast services until the introduction of the Class 90s. Progressively withdrawn from 2003 onwards, many were sold to Bulgaria for further service. Sporting the InterCity sector livery that replaced the drab rail blue, No. 87012 leaves London Euston for Glasgow in October 1986. In steam days this working would have been the Down Mid-Day Scot. No. 87012 was exported to Bulgaria in 2007.

The High Speed Train

The rising competition from the motorways led the cash-strapped railways to develop a prototype HST in 1972.

The production result was a diesel-electric-powered train with a power car at each end developing 2,250 hp, with seven or eight Mk III carriages in between. Capable of sustained speeds of 125 mph, it achieved a world record-breaking speed of 143 mph in June 1973, which still stands.

The InterCity 125 trains entered service on the Great Western Main Line from London Paddington to Bristol and South Wales in the autumn of 1976. Later trains were introduced on the Great Northern in May 1978. The trains also starting operating on the Midland main line from St Pancras as well as on cross-country services. Still in widespread use, the first withdrawals are imminent with the introduction of the new Class 800 electro-diesel trains and the Class 801 electric multiple units.

No. 43042

No. 43042 sports a hybrid livery – the InterCity sector livery and the old blue/grey – as it rests over at London King's Cross in August 1986.

The 1980s – The Woodhead Debacle

This decade produced what many observers would regard as the most politically motivated piece of managerial stupidity the railway industry had seen for a long time.

The LNER/Great Central Woodhead route was a key freight line linking Manchester and Sheffield under the Pennines via the Woodhead Tunnel. Steam-hauled operation was difficult and the LNER planned electrification in 1936. Delayed by the Second World War, the electrification at 1,500 volts DC was eventually completed in 1955. The line was closed to passenger traffic in 1970, and with the decline in coal traffic across the Pennines, and being deemed non-standard, the line was closed in 1981, with the tracks being lifted.

The tunnels have been used to carry cables by the National Grid. The line remains open and electrified at 25 kV AC from Manchester to Hadfield. The line is also open from Penistone to Barnsley Junction.

Proposals to reopen the link have not materialised. Other trans-Pennine electrification projects are under consideration.

Two types of electric locomotive were built to operate the services.

Class 76 No. 26020 (No. 76020), (LNER EM1), Bo-Bo, 1,500 Volt DC

The first locomotive was built at Doncaster in 1941. Between 1947 and 1952 it was loaned to Netherlands Railways and acquired the name *Tommy*. Eventually, a further fifty-seven locomotives were built. The untimely closure of the Woodhead line in 1981 rendered the entire class redundant. Despite still being serviceable and in excellent condition, and despite an offer being received from Netherlands Railways to buy them, political bloody-mindedness prevailed and the locomotives were scrapped. One was saved for preservation and is seen as part of the Rainhill cavalcade in May 1980. Seven Class EM2 locomotives were also constructed to work passenger services over the Woodhead route. The class was withdrawn in 1968 and was eventually sold to Netherlands Railways.

New Trains

On the positive side, the 1980s saw considerable investment in new rolling stock.

Electric Multiple Units

Above: Class 315 No. 315842, 25 kV

Built at York in 1980, the Class 315s have operated the Great Eastern suburban services out of London Liverpool Street to Gidea Park, Shenfield, Chingford and the Lea Valley. Still operational, they are due to be replaced in 2018 by the new Class 710s on the West Anglia services and the Shenfield line by the Crossrail Class 345, which began to come into service as of summer 2017. No. 315842 sports the new Network SouthEast colours as it accelerates onto the Ilford flyover with a Liverpool Street working in December 1986.

Left: Class 317 No. 317319, 25 kV

Built at York in two batches in 1981–2 and 1985–7, the first batch of Class 317s was built for the newly electrified London St Pancras–Bedford (BEDPAN) service. Entry into service was delayed by a protracted industrial dispute over one-man operated (OMO) trains. Displaced in 1987 by the dual-voltage Class 319, they were sent to operate out of Euston before eventually joining the later built batch on the Great Northern and West Anglia routes. They now operate on the Lea Valley services out of London Liverpool Street and Stratford. They will be replaced by the Classes 710 and 720 in 2018/19. No. 317319 is dwarfed by the Barbican Centre as it pauses at Barbican on a Moorgate (widened lines) service to Luton.

Class 318 No. 318268, 25 kV

Built at York in 1985–6 to serve the newly electrified Glasgow & South Western lines to Ayr and Largs, the Class 318s were refurbished in 2005–7 and are still in service. They are currently undergoing a life-extension refurbishment in Doncaster. No. 318268 waits at Largs to return to Glasgow – 'Away ta Gleska' – in August 1988.

Class 319 No. 319012, 25 kV/750 Volt DC (Third Rail)

Built in two batches at York for the new cross-London Thameslink service from Bedford to Brighton, the Class 319s remained on this corridor until the introduction of new trains in 2015, at which point some were deployed for use elsewhere. No. 319012 sports the new Network SouthEast livery as it pauses at King's Cross (Thameslink) on a northbound service in June 1988.

Class 321 No. 321309, 25 kV

Three batches of Class 321 units were built at York from 1988 to 1991. The initial batch (Class 321/3) appeared on the Great Eastern lines, replacing life-expired slam-door stock and to operate new electric services to Ipswich and Harwich. Still in service, they are due for a major refurbishment and upgrade.

The second batch (Class 321/4) went initially to the West Coast lines out of Euston, operating as far as Birmingham. Later, some of this batch joined the 321/3 on the Great Eastern. Between 2010 and 2015, some saw service on the Great Northern out of King's Cross.

The final batch (Class 321/9) went to the West Yorkshire PTE to work between Leeds and Doncaster. Now operated by Northern Rail, they remain in service, but are due to be replaced by the new Class 331 units in 2019. Although some units will receive major upgrades, many will be replaced by the Class 720s in 2019. No. 321309 is captured outside Ilford (Seven Kings) car sheds, having recently been delivered from York.

Class 442 (5 WES) No. 442401

In 1988 twenty-four Class 442 (5 WES) (Wessex) units were built at Derby to operate on the newly electrified Waterloo–Weymouth services. In 2007 they were transferred to the Gatwick Express service. Withdrawn from that in 2016, they will reappear on the Waterloo–Portsmouth service in 2018. Regarded as some of the most reliable and successful EMUs, the class holds the world speed record for a third-rail EMU at 108 mph. No. 442401 is seen as it approaches Southampton on a test run in April 1988.

Class 455/7-9, 750 Volt DC (Third Rail)

These units were built at York for the Southern Region third-rail network in the early to mid-1980s to operate on the inner suburban services. Class 455/8 No. 455861 passes Mortlake in May 1987.

Class 141 Pacer No. 141003

This was the first production model of the Pacer DMU. It was a cheap option, based upon the successful Leyland National single-decker bus, to replace life-expired first generation DMUs. Initially ordered in 1984 for the West Yorkshire PTE, they proved unreliable, notoriously noisy and extremely rough riders, although later modification rectified some of the problems. All were withdrawn in 1997 and some were exported to Iran in 2001/2. No. 141003 is observed at York sporting the initial West Yorkshire PTE Verona green/buttermilk livery. This unit was scrapped following an accident in 1989.

Class 142 Pacer No. 142020

The Class 142 Pacer was a development of the earlier Class 141 built at Derby in 1985–87 for rural branch lines. Found unsuitable for the sharp curves on the Cornish branch lines, most have been employed around major cities in the north of England and Cardiff. Still in service, complete withdrawal is expected by 2019. No. 142020 sports a mock Great Western chocolate and cream livery as it arrives at Keighley in April 1988.

Class 143 Pacer No. 143025

Built between 1985 and 1986, the body of the Class 143 Pacer is clearly based upon a bus design. After initially working in the north of England, they have since been transferred to South Wales and the South West, where they work around Cardiff and Exeter. Accessibility legislation means that they will be withdrawn by the end of 2018. No. 143025 sports the Tyneside PTE livery as it leaves Newcastle-upon-Tyne in July 1988.

Class 144 Pacer No. 144022

Built 1986–87 and allocated to the West Yorkshire PTE (branded Metro), the Class 144 Pacers were originally painted in the crimson/cream livery. Now operated by Northern Rail, they are scheduled for withdrawal at the end of 2019. No. 144022 is caught at Knaresborough in September 1987.

Class 150 Sprinter

Built at York in three batches to replace life-expired heritage units, the Class 150 Sprinters marked a return to Voith hydraulic transmission. Prototype Class 150/0 was followed by production Classes 150/1 and 150/2. The prototypes remained in service in the Midlands until 2011, when they were transferred to Great Western, refurbished, and are now used on the Reading–Basingstoke service. The Class 150/1 was introduced in 1985–6 and most are still in service in the West Country, the Midlands and the north of England. The Class 150/2 was introduced in 1976–78 and is fitted with front-end connections for longer services. Again, most are still in service in Wales, the West Country and the north of England.

Prototype No. 150001 (*above*) loads for Birmingham at Worcester (Foregate Street) station in September 1990; No. 150131 (*middle*) is seen at Crewe, ready to depart for Shrewsbury in July 1987; and No. 150258 (*below*) arrives at York on a Scarborough–Liverpool (Lime Street) service in September 1987.

Class 155 Sprinter No. 155238

Built by Leyland Bus between 1987 and 1988, using mainly bus components, Class 155 Sprinter units replaced aging diesel-mechanical units. The unsuitability of the Pacer units on many rural branches with tight curves led to their conversion to single-car Class 153s for working in Cornwall, Wales, the North West and East Anglia. The seven remaining units had been allocated to and remain with the West Yorkshire PTE. No. 155238 prepares to leave Cardiff (Central) for Manchester in December 1988.

Class 156 Supersprinter No. 156503

These two-car units were built in 1988 by Metro-Cammell in Birmingham to replace life-expired first generation DMUs and locomotive-hauled trains. They have operated extensively throughout all parts of the UK. Some of the Scottish units worked the long journey from Glasgow to Fort William and Mallaig. All remain in service with the privatised operating companies. Brand-new No. 156503 proudly sports the Strathclyde orange/black livery as it is about to depart from Glasgow (Queen Street) for Cumbernauld.

Class 58 No. 58027, Co-Co, Diesel-Electric, 3,300 hp

This was a low-cost, easily maintained freight locomotive for the predicted growing freight market of the 1980s. They were also designed for the export market and differed in construction and subsequent maintenance by being totally modular. Fifty locomotives were introduced into service from 1982 to 1987. The final locomotive entered service in 1987, and was the last diesel locomotive to be built at the Doncaster plant. Performance and availability was disappointing, export orders did not materialise and the miners' strike reduced many of their coal hauling duties. Supplanted by the new and more reliable Class 66, most are now stored or operational on European construction projects.

No. 58027 brings a loaded MGR coal train eastbound through Nottingham (Midland) in August 1988. No. 58027 had entered service in March 1985 and was withdrawn in September 1999, being exported to Europe in October 2004.

Class 59 No. 59003 *Yeoman Highlander,* Co-Co, Diesel-Electric, 3,300 hp

Quarry owner and operator Foster Yeoman were totally dissatisfied with the poor standard of reliability and availably of the Class 56s working their stone trains from the West Country to London. Following the success of their own internal EMD SW1001 shunter, the Class 59/0s were designed, developed and ordered from the US Electro-Motive Diesel, with the first arriving in January 1986. They were the first privately owned locomotives to operate on British Railways. The Class 59 has consistently achieved better than the projected 95 per cent availability and reliability, and in 1991 set a European single loco freight haulage record: a 5,415-foot-long train weighing 11,982 tons.

No. 59003 was delivered in 1986. It operated Yeoman's stone trains until it was sold to Germany in 1997. Repatriated in 2014, it was purchased by GB Railfreight, and it now operates from their Peterborough base. The locomotive is seen while on display at the Basingstoke open day in July 1987.

Class 90 No. 90004, Bo-Bo, 5,000 hp

The Class 90s were built at Crewe from 1987 to 1990 for express passenger and heavy freight work to replace the aging Classes 81–85 on the West Coast Main Line out of Euston. The onset of sectorisation, and ultimately privatisation, led to division between the sectors. After a period with Virgin Trains, the passenger locomotives now work the Great Eastern services to Norwich under the Abellio Greater Anglia franchise. Others are divided between DB Cargo UK and Freightliner, while eleven are currently stored and two have been withdrawn. No. 90004 sports the new InterCity sector 'Swallow' livery at Glasgow (Central) in August 1988.

Class 89 No. 89001 *Avocet*, Co-Co, 6,000 hp

No. 89001 is seen sporting InterCity livery as it leaves King's Cross on the 17.36 to Peterborough in August 1988. A prototype locomotive built at Crewe but designed by Brush Traction at Loughborough, it first ran on 20 February 1987. After a chequered career, it is now in the care of the AC Locomotive Group at Barrow Hill, where it is undergoing a long and expensive restoration.

Class 91 No. 91004, Bo-Bo, 6,480 hp

After thirty-four years, and two generations of diesel power, the promised East Coast electrification finally materialised. The Class 91s were built at Crewe and are theoretically capable of 225 kph (140 mph). They were originally described as the InterCity 225. They entered service in March 1989 and one of the locomotives, No. 91010, achieved a record 161.7 mph on a test run down Stoke Bank in September 1989, thirty-five years after a French 1,500 volt DC electric locomotive achieved 151 mph, which is still a record for a British locomotive. Now operated by Virgin Trains East Coast, all are still in service. No. 91004 is captured on test, pausing at Grantham in August 1988.

Sectors

As the 1980s progressed, the railways moved from their traditional regional basis into Sectors – with branding, serious attempts at marketing and image projection. Passenger brands appeared, such as the relaunch of InterCity, the appearance of London & South East, which quickly evolved into Network SouthEast, Regional Railways and ScotRail. Freight reappeared under Rail Express Systems (for mail and parcels), Trainload Freight (where there were block coal or oil trains), Freightliner (for containers) and Speedlink. Cynics will call it a bonanza for the paint and vinyl manufacturers!

Class 86/1 No. 86103 *Andre Chapelon*

No. 86103 heads out of Birmingham (New Street) with the northbound 'Clansman' in September 1988. Built in 1966, it was withdrawn in 1995 after twenty-nine years of service and was eventually scrapped in 2002.

London & South East

This brand eventually evolved into Network SouthEast, but not before it sported the almost legendary 'Jaffa Cake' livery, which began to appear in 1986. The creation of Network SouthEast with its charismatic and highly successful manager, Chris Green, saw it replaced by the blue/white/red/grey 'toothpaste' livery.

Class 309 No. 309613

The Class 309 'Clacton Express' units were built in 1962–63. They were the first 25 kV express units and the first units capable of 100 mph. Progressively replaced by the very inferior Class 321/3 units in 1989, they continued until 1992, being downgraded to rush hour-only services until January 1994, when they were finally withdrawn. Seven units were sent to work around the Manchester area from 1994–2002. These final units were withdrawn and scrapped in 2004. No. 309613 sports Jaffa Cake livery as it passes through Harold Wood (Essex) on a Down working in November 1986.

No. 309606

No. 309606 sports the later livery as it arrives at London (Liverpool Street) in January 1994. The pantograph above the cab indicates that this was once a two-car unit, recalling the days of ten-car operation. For the technical, this is an evening shot, hand-held with my trusty Olympus and using 1000ASA film.

Regional Railways
Regional Railways eventually settled for shades of blue.

No. 47475

No. 47475 sports the blue and white livery with the light blue stripe at Manchester (Victoria) in March 1989. No. 47475 entered service in July 1964 and was withdrawn in January 2003. ScotRail favoured a variation on the InterCity livery but with a light blue band. The band was at the same level as on the carriages.

No. 47714 *Grampian Region*

Complete with Eastfield 'Scotty Dog' motif, No. 47714 prepares to depart from Glasgow (Queen Street) for Aberdeen. No. 47714 entered traffic in November 1966 and was converted to operate on the push-pull services from Glasgow to Edinburgh and Aberdeen in 1985. It is still operational.

Railfreight

Railfreight moved first to an all-over grey, then to an attractive large logo grey with a red sole bar.

Left and right: No. 56049

No. 56049 is fresh out of the Crewe paint shops, sporting this pleasing livery. The locomotive is still in service with Colas Rail. Railfreight then moved to an attractive two-tone grey with colourful sector symbols. Although sporting the wavy lines to suggest petroleum products, 1962-built No. 37717 and partner haul empty iron ore gondolas from Llanwern steelworks through Cardiff en route for Port Talbot on a sunny afternoon in September 1989. No. 37717 was withdrawn in 2004 after forty-two years of service.

No. 58012 *Didcot Power Station*

Sporting the black diamonds for the coal sector, No. 58012 races with empty coal hoppers through Oxford en route from Didcot back to Nottinghamshire in August 1988. Rail Express Systems handled the mail and parcels. The livery was a pleasing Post Office red with grey and a motif. The locomotives were often seen idle during the day between night-time activities.

No. 86417

Seen under the historic Victorian roof of Rugby station in July 2000, No. 86417 was built in 1966 and was withdrawn in September 2001.

The 1990s

New Trains

Diesel Multiple Units

Class 153 No. 153380

In the early 1990s the need was recognised for a single-carriage DMU for rural branch lines. It was decided in 1991–92 to split thirty-five of the two-car Class 155 units to form seventy single-car Class 153 units. No. 153380 pauses at Pantyffynon (Co. Dyfed) on a southbound Central Wales Line working in September 1998.

Above and below: Class 158/159 Express Sprinter

A total of 182 Class 158 units were built at Derby to replace elderly first generation DMUs and expensive locomotive-hauled services. Most are two-car sets, but some three-car sets were built for the West Yorkshire PTE. The first units entered service from Edinburgh Haymarket in 1990. The Class 159 was built specially for the former Southern Region route to Exeter via Salisbury. The main difference is the more powerful 400 hp Cummins diesel.

No. 158767 (*above*) sports the Regional Railways livery and Express logo at Bristol (Temple Meads) in June 1991, while NSE-liveried No. 159014 (*below*) prepares to leave London for Exeter (St David's) in May 1993.

Class 165 Network Turbo

Built in 1990–92 for the Thames and Chiltern division of Network SouthEast to replace life-expired first generation DMUs and locomotive-hauled trains operating out of Paddington and Marylebone.

Class 165 No. 165024

No. 165024 waits at Aylesbury to return to London Marylebone in June 1992. This was part of the former Great Central Railway joint line with the Metropolitan.

Class 165 No. 165109

No. 165109 powers through Sonning Cutting (Berks) towards Paddington in September 1992.

Class 168 Networker No. 168004

Built in 1997 for Chiltern Railways services from London to the Midlands, Class 186s have the distinction of being the first units ordered post-privatisation. No. 168004 waits at Banbury with a Marylebone service in August 2000.

Class 170 Turbostar

Class 170 No. 170103

Between 1998 and 2005, 122 Class 170 units were built to work regional and long-distance services. No. 170103 sports the Midland Mainline franchise livery at London St Pancras in March 1999.

Class 320 No. 320316, 25 kV

The Class 320 is a three-car version of the Class 321 specially adapted for the needs of the Strathclyde PTE, built in 1990 to replace elderly Class 303 and 311 units. No. 320316 leaves Airdrie (An t-Àrd Ruigh if you prefer!) for Drumgelloch on the former North British line from Glasgow (Queen Street) to Edinburgh. This line was completely closed in 1982, but reopened and electrified initially to Drumgelloch. The line was later reopened through to Edinburgh to provide a fourth route between the two cities. The single track shown in this April 1993 picture was doubled as part of the reopening project.

Class 321/9 No. 321902

The final batch of three Class 321 units was introduced in 1991 and specifically dedicated to the West Yorkshire PTE to work the busy Leeds–Doncaster corridor. No. 321902 arrives at Doncaster in March 1992.

Class 322 No. 322481, Stansted Express, 25 kV

The Class 322s are a class of five units that were initially dedicated to the London (Liverpool Street) to Stansted Airport service. After being rendered surplus on this route they passed in turn to various operators, and they now work around Leeds as part of the West Yorkshire PTE fleet. They will eventually be replaced by CAF-built Class 331 units. No. 322481 approaches the Stansted Airport terminal having come along the new branch line from the Great Eastern London–Cambridge main line. The branch line is entirely new and was not built over either the old Thaxted branch or the closed Dunmow–Braintree line.

Class 325 No. 325105, 25 kV/750 Volt DC Postal Units

Built at Derby in 1995–96 to handle postal traffic, they operated until the Royal Mail withdrew the contracts in 2003. The contracts passed to GBRf and eventually to DB Schenker in 2010. They are largely confined to working the West Coast and East Coast Main Line routes. No. 325015 forms 1M44 Tonbridge–Willesden as it passes through Kensington Olympia in the late 1990s.

Class 332 No. 332006, Heathrow Express, 25 kV

The fourteen Class 332s, which were initially four-car units but were extended to five, were built by CAF at Zaragoza, Spain, in 1997–98 for the Paddington–Heathrow express service. Seen here is No. 332006, which is waiting to leave Paddington early in February 1998.

Class 333 No. 333003, 25 kV

Sixteen Class 333 units were built by Siemens and CAF in Zaragoza in 1999–2000 for service with the West Yorkshire Metro. Although capable of 100 mph, the routes the serve are limited to 90 mph. Now operated by Northern Rail, No. 333003 is seen at Skipton in August 2003. (Railwaymedia)

Class 365 No. 365532, 25 kV/750 Volts DC

Forty-one units were built at York in 1994–95. They have the dubious distinction of being the last units built at York. No. 365532 still sports the NSE livery as it emerges from Welwyn North Tunnel in August 1999.

New Third-Rail Units

Class 456 No. 456006, Two-Car EMU, 750 Volts DC (Third Rail)

Twenty-four units were built at York to replace life-expired Class 416 (2EPB) units. The grey on their Network SouthEast livery seemed darker than on other trains. They also share the same body style as the Class 320–322 family. Since privatisation, they have worked for the Connex, Southern and South West Trains franchises. No. 456006 had just been delivered to Clapham Junction when seen in May 1991.

Class 458 Juniper 4JOP No. 458024

Thirty units were built for South West Trains in 1998 for outer suburban services. Initially notoriously unreliable, perseverance paid off and the problems were rectified and reliability was substantially improved.

Above and below: Class 460 8GAT

Eight units were built in 1999–2001 exclusively for the Gatwick Express service until they were withdrawn in 2012. They have been converted into Class 458/5 units to work for South West Trains. A rare shot, No. 460001 (*above*) is seen in works undercoat and without its Darth Vader nose cone while on test at Horsham in November 1999. Meanwhile, No. 460002 (*below*), complete with its Darth Vader 'Gatwick Zephyr' nose cone, speeds through Clapham Junction en route for Gatwick Airport in July 2006.

Class 465 Networker, 750 Volts DC

The Networker came in two formats: diesel-hydraulic units, for the former Great Western and Chiltern services, and electric, for the former Southern routes into Kent. Newly delivered No. 465001 is seen at Strawberry Hill.

Class 466 Networker, 750 Volt Dc

Class 466 Networkers were two-car units built in 1993–94 to work with Class 465s. A Class 466 is captured as the lead unit at Woolwich Dockyard in March 1993.

Class 59/1 No. 59104

Amey Roadstone emulated Foster Yeoman and acquired its own locomotives from the United States. No. 59104 *Village of Great Elm* returns empty stone hoppers to the West Country through West Drayton in July 1991.

Class 60 No. 60029 *Ben Nevis*, Co-Co

Introduced in 1990, the Class 60 locomotives replaced a lot of expensive double-heading, particularly in south-east England and South Wales. Unreliable Class 56s and 58s were also replaced on some workings. An example of replaced double-heading can be seen here, as No. 60029 returns empty iron ore gondolas through Cardiff en route from Llanwern steelworks to the ore terminal at Port Talbot in September 1991.

PTE Progress

West Yorkshire

No. 307130

The expansion of the electrified suburban lines around Leeds meant that West Yorkshire had to rely on cascaded life-expired Class 307 units. Resplendent in its new West Yorkshire Metro livery (its fifth!), thirty-four-year-old No. 307130 waits in Ilford car sheds to be transferred north in August 1990.

Above and below: Class 507/8

Merseyrail had been a little more fortunate. Relatively modern Class 507 No. 507008 (*above*) runs into Kirkdale en route to Liverpool (Exchange) in March 1998. The Merseyrail electrification was also extended to Chester, and Class 508 No. 508102 (*below*) passes Hooton-on-Wirral on a Chester–Liverpool (Exchange) service in October 1993.

Class 150 No. 150117

Things are looking up on the non-electrified part of the West Midlands PTE network. Class 150 No. 150117 has just arrived at Birmingham (New Street) from Kidderminster in July 1991.

Above and below: No. 308136

Elsewhere, all was not completely well. Delays on the electrification and delivery of new trains on the Lichfield–Redditch cross-city line meant reliance on clapped-out combinations of first generation DMUs and cascades from the London area. Still in NSE livery, but reduced to three coaches, No. 308136 (*above*) waits at Longbridge before returning to Lichfield in September 1993. Even worse, No. 308158 (*below*) sports the West Yorkshire livery as it arrives at Barnt Green on a Lichfield–Redditch service in November 1994.

Class 323 No. 323211

Eventually, the Class 323 units were delivered from the manufacturer. Lichfield-bound No. 323211 pauses at Barnt Green en route to Lichfield while No. 323215 waits to enter the single line section to Redditch in November 1994.

Greater Manchester

A combination of a decline in traffic in the Strathclyde area in the 1980s, and the conversion of the Hadfield/Glossop line to 25 kV, led to a number of Class 303 units being cascaded to Greater Manchester.

No. 303060

In the similar but less striking Great Manchester livery, No. 303060 loads up at Altrincham in August 1989. These units were withdrawn in the mid-1990s.

No. 305410

Manchester also suffered from the late delivery of the Class 323s. With the red strip and NSE sticker removed, exiled No. 305410 leaves Manchester (Piccadilly) for Glossop in November 1994.

No. 32323o

No. 32323o waits to leave Manchester (Piccadilly) for the airport in November 1994.

Metrolink

Eventually, Manchester went down the light rail, or 'Tram Train', route as it was deemed the least expensive rail-based option. Approval was given in 1988 and the first services began between Manchester (Victoria) and Bury in April 1992. The highly successful network now consists of seven lines totalling 57 route miles and carries over 37 million passengers every year.

No. 1019

The Bury route had been electrified by the Lancashire & Yorkshire Railway in 1916 using a 1,200 volt DC third-rail system. This remained in place until the light rail takeover in 1992. No. 1019 is seen approaching Heaton Park in May 1998. The profusion of late spring blossom made the picture irresistible.

Freight Operators

Railfreight Progress

Under the Railways Act 1993, Railfreight was split into shadow franchises – Loadhaul Ltd, Mainline Freight and Transrail Freight.

No. 56102 sports the attractive Loadhaul black/orange livery as it works train 6E86, Ripple Lane–Immingham, through Canonbury in November 1998. By this time, Loadhaul had become part of English, Welsh & Scottish Railway (EWS). No. 56102 entered service in 1981 and, after only twenty-two years of service, was withdrawn in 2003.

Nos 37077/046

Nos 37077/046 bring gravel hoppers through Stratford. No. 37077 sports the Mainline Freight blue livery, which, with the silver stripe, looked particularly good on the Class 37s. It is June 1997, and Mainline had already become part of EWS. Built in 1962, both locomotives saw forty-six years of service.

No. 56052 *The Cardiff Rod Mill*

Sporting the somewhat subdued Transrail livery – essentially a sticker over what was already in place – No. 56052 is in charge of 6C32, the Cwmgwrach–Aberthaw coal working, as it passes through Pyle in September 1997. No. 56052 had clocked thirty years of service when withdrawn in 2008.

English, Welsh & Scottish Railway

From February 1996, the various freight operators were absorbed into English, Welsh & Scottish Railway (EWS).

No. 56041

Sporting the distinctive and not unattractive red and gold livery, complete with the lion, dragon and stag (Beasties) motif as it works the daily Bow–Heck working through Stratford in April 1997, No. 56041 was withdrawn in 2003 after twenty-five years of service.

No. 66012 Class 66 Co-Co

The new American owners of English, Welsh & Scottish Railway were confronted with a problem – aged Class 37s and 47s, unreliable and frequently unavailable Class 56 and 58, and the jury still out on the Class 60s demanded that drastic action was taken in the form of an order for 250 Class 60 locomotives from General Motors. No. 66012 was the first I saw, bringing the 7V58 Harlow–Acton train over the third rail electrified No. 2 lines through sylvan Canonbury (North London) on 18 November 1998.

No. 59206

Eventually, EWS was taken over by Deutsche Bahn in the form of DB Schenker. No. 59206 is seen in the new German red livery bringing the 6V18 Hither Green–Whatley train through Lewisham in October 2009.

The Channel Tunnel Link

One of the two main highlights of the 1990s was the opening of the Channel Tunnel and the direct rail link initially from Waterloo to Paris and Brussels.

With the classic backdrop of Battersea Power Station, No. 3015 leads a London–Brussels service through Wandsworth Road in August 1995.

Class 92, Co-Co, 25 kV, 6,760 hp/750 Volt DC (Third Rail), 5,360 hp

With high expectations of considerable volumes of freight traffic, and even overnight sleeper services, through the Channel Tunnel, forty-six dual-voltage locomotives were built by Brush/ASEA Brown Boveri in 1993–6. Reality proved to be way below the blue-sky dreams and expectations, with nine of the locomotives now working in Romania, four in Bulgaria and six being allocated to the Caledonian Sleeper services. No. 92023 *Ravel* is in the Kent countryside, passing Borough Green and Wrotham with the 7O58 Dagenham–Dollands Moor–Spain train in May 1995. At present, all freight goes down the old route to the tunnel. No. 92023 is also on the Caledonian Sleeper service.

No. 9013, Co-Co

Like the Eurostar passenger service, the Shuttle is another Channel Tunnel success story. Built by Brush and based on the lessons learned from No. 89001, these locomotives work the trains carrying cars, coaches and trucks through the tunnel from Dollands Moor to Calais. (Derek Warrick)

Rail Privatisation

The second major highlight of the 1990s was rail privatisation under the provisions of the Railways Act 1993. Initially, even the infrastructure was placed under Railtrack, although this was to prove short-lived, with everything returning to public ownership by 2004. The passenger operation is worked through franchises, while freight came under the American-owned English, Welsh & Scottish Railway and Freightliner, although other operators later appeared on the scene.

The initial franchisees inherited whatever stock was available, and it was a while before new stock began to appear.

The following photographs clearly show that, once again, the only real winners were the paint and vinyl manufacturers.

Virgin

Virgin acquired two franchises – the West Coast Main Line and cross-country services, under the name Virgin CrossCountry. The latter was operated until 2007.

Above and below: No. 43083 and No. 86244 *Royal British Legion*

No. 43083 (*above*) sports the striking Virgin CrossCountry livery as it leads the 17.02 departure from Sheffield for Plymouth in August 1997 while 1965-built No. 86244 *Royal British Legion* (*below*) starts 1S87 away from Preston on 11 July 2001. The locomotive was withdrawn the following year.

Great Western Trains/First Great Western

Originally beginning operation in February 1996, Great Western Trains became part of First Great Western in 1998. The current franchise has recently been extended to 2020.

No. 43016/126

No. 43016/126 approaches Tiverton sporting the original privatisation livery in August 1998.

First Great Eastern

First Great Eastern was the initial franchise that operated the Great Eastern suburban services out of Liverpool Street to Gidea Park and Shenfield, as well as services to Southend-on-Sea and Colchester. Despite dramatically improving the Shenfield services, the franchise was lost after only seven years in 2004.

No. 321439

No. 321439 sports the First Great Eastern livery at Southend-on-Sea in October 1997.

South West Trains

Owned by bus company Stagecoach, South West Trains successfully operated the territory of the former London & South Western Railway as far as Exeter. Stagecoach successfully retained the franchise in 2004, but sadly lost it despite a commitment and delivery of more new trains in 2017.

No. 411566 (4CEP)

Originally built in 1956–63 as part of the Kent electrification, 4CEP unit No. 411566 sports the stylish Stagecoach livery as it arrives at Brockenhurst from Lymington in April 1998.

Connex

Connex initially operated two franchises: South Eastern (broadly the former South Eastern & Chatham Railway) and South Central (broadly the former London, Brighton & South Coast network). The latter franchise lasted from 1996 to 2001. Connex was stripped of its franchise two and a half years before it was due to expire. It was the first operator to lose a franchise.

Nos 319214 and 319218

Nos 319214 and 319218 approach Clapham Junction in February 1997.

Central Trains

Between 1997 and 2007 Central Trains operated regional services radiating from Birmingham, as well as local services around the Midlands and Birmingham suburban services.

No. 158791

No. 158791 is working a Norwich–Birmingham (New Street) service when seen departing from Thetford (Norfolk) in February 2004.

Anglia Railways

Operated from January 1997 to March 2004, Anglia Railways operated the Great Eastern Main Line from London Liverpool Street to Norwich and branch services within East Anglia. One major advantage was the introduction of a half-hourly inter-city service from London to Norwich.

No. 86237 *University of East Anglia*

No. 86237 *University of East Anglia* (formerly West Coast *Sir Charles Halle*) sports its fine new livery as it propels a Down Norwich express into Ipswich in January 1999.

Silverlink

Silverlink was created to cover the North London lines, the West London line, the Euston–Watford DC lines and the Gospel Oak to Barking (GOBLIN) line. Silverlink County also covered services to Northampton, St Albans (Abbey) and the Bletchley–Bedford line. The franchise lasted from 1997 to 2007.

No. 313103

No. 313103 is seen on the West London line at West Brompton, with Earl's Court in the background in July 1999. This was a big improvement to the hitherto 'Kenny Belle' service from Clapham Junction to Kensington Olympia.

Into the Twenty-First Century

In this section we will monitor the introduction of new trains and further investment. The freight business changed dramatically, with several major operators on the scene.

New Trains

Diesel Multiple Units

Class 170 No. 170304

The Class 170/3 Turbostar DMU was introduced in 2000 by South West Trains to supplement their Class 159 units, and No. 170304 runs into Basingstoke on a very wet February day in 2001.

Class 172 No. 172004

No. 172004 is one of the new diesel units introduced by TfL for the Gospel Oak–Barking Line (GOBLIN) prior to electrification. The promised electrification is under construction, albeit over a year late. No. 172004 approaches Leytonstone in July 2017. The catenary masts are in position.

Class 172/2 No. 172216

The Class 172/2 is a variation on the Class 170 Turbostar family that is fitted with corridor connections between units. No. 172216 forms part of a Birmingham (Snow Hill)–Knowle & Dorridge service on a summer's evening in June 2015.

Class 175 No. 175004

Built by Alstom at Washwood Heath in 1999–2001 and sporting First North Western livery, No. 175004 pauses at Stafford on a Birmingham–Crewe–Holyhead working in July 2001.

Class 180 Coradia/Adelante

Built by Alstom in 2000–01, the Class 180 Coradia/Adelantes have had a chequered history. No. 180111 is seen in Cardiff with the 15.30 Great Western working from Paddington on a very wet August afternoon in 2002.

Class 185 Desiro

These 100 mph units were built by Siemens at Krefeld for the First Trans-Peninne Express franchise. No. 185139 forms the 12.50 departure from Barnetby (Lincs) to Manchester Airport in June 2009.

Class 220 Voyager No. 220017

The Class 220 was Virgin's response for the CrossCountry services. Brand-new Virgin Voyager No. 220017 is seen passing Leamington Spa on test in June 2001.

Class 334 Juniper, 25 kV

Built by Alstom between 2000 and 2003 for the Strathclyde outer suburban services, the Class 334 Junipers were initially used on the Clyde Coast services. They are now found operating the Helensburgh–Edinburgh via Bathgate and the Dalmiur–Lanark routes. No. 334033 is seen sporting the Strathclyde 'blood and custard' livery as it arrives at Ayr on a very wet July day in 2003.

Class 350 Desiro, 25 kV (350/1, 750 Volt DC)

Built by Siemens in batches from 2004 onwards, these 100 mph units work on the West Coast Main Line for the London Midland franchise, but the Class 350/4s are inter-city units for the Trans-Pennine Express Manchester–Scotland services. No. 350242 is seen at Watford in May 2009.

Class 357 Electrostar, 25 kV EMU

Old, out-dated and unreliable rolling stock earned the former London, Tilbury & Southend route out of London's Fenchurch Street the reputation of being the 'misery line' until new trains appeared in 2001. No. 357204 is seen in the yard at Shoeburyness (Essex) in September 2001.

Class 375 Electrostar, 750 Volt DC

No. 375617 is the lead unit on an Up Ramsgate–London (Victoria) service as it passes Wandsworth Road on a wet June evening in 2001.

Class 376 Electrostar, 750 Volt DC

These rather bland-looking units were built by Bombardier in Derby in 2004 for the South Eastern inner suburban commuter services. Here, No. 376022 stands at London Charing Cross in the evening rush hour in March 2005.

Class 377 and 379 Electrostar, 25 kV/750 Volt DC EMU

The most numerous type of EMU, with 211 units having been constructed by Bombardier at Derby since 2001, they currently operate with Southeastern, Southern and Thameslink franchises. No. 377508 is a 377/5 dual-voltage unit built for Thameslink and is seen entering East Croydon on a Bedford–Brighton service in November 2009. Class 700 units have begun to supersede these units on the Thameslink services.

Class 378 No. 378146

After years of battling against closure, TfL finally invested in the North London line to recreate an outer circle of suburban services. No. 378146 is seen on the reopened Dalston to Shoreditch section in April 2010. The trains have since been extended to five cars and now operate a weekend all-night service.

Class 380 No. 380004 Desiro, 25 kV

The Class 380 Desiros were built in 2010 by Siemens for ScotRail services in Ayrshire, Renfrewshire and Inverclyde. Three-car unit No. 380004 is captured at Ayr. (D. Burrell)

Class 387/2 Electrostar No. 387208, 25 kV 750 Volts DC

The Class 387 was introduced in 2014 with the Class 387/2 specifically designed for the Gatwick Express service. Designed for one-man operation (OMO), they have been the centre of a protracted and acrimonious dispute over the safety of OMO operation on twelve-car trains. This has seen the unhappy combination of union bloody-mindedness and managerial and political incompetence at its worst. No. 387208 is the lead unit, approaching East Croydon on a Gatwick-bound working in September 2016.

Class 390 Pendolino No. 390020, 25 kV EMU

Class 390 Pendolinos were the star trains of the privatisation era, and Virgin West Coast commissioned fifty-three nine-car units for the services out of London Euston. Using Fiat Ferroviaria tilting train technology, they are capable of 140 mph, making them some of the fastest EMUs operating within the United Kingdom. In 2006 one unit ran the 401 miles from Glasgow Central to Euston in a record-breaking three hours fifty-five minutes. Recalling the pre-war streamlined trains in both colour and style, No. 390020 is seen waiting to leave Euston with the 16.20 to Manchester in April 2003.

Class 395 Javelin, 25 kV 750 Volt DC

Built in 2009 to provide a high-speed commuter service from St Pancras into Kent using the Channel Tunnel high-speed line, many Class 395 Javelins are named for successful Olympic athletes. No. 395006 *Daley Thompson* runs into Ebbsfleet with a St Pancras–Faversham working on Trafalgar Day 2017.

Class 444 Desiro No. 444026, 750 Volt DC

Built by Siemens in 2002–04 for South West Trains, and capable of 100 mph, these highly successful and reliable trains operate the inter-city services from London to Portsmouth, Southampton and Bournemouth. No. 444026 is in the classic Waterloo pose as it forms the 14.38 service to Portsmouth Harbour in August 2004.

Class 450 Desiro No. 450012 (4-DES), 750 Volt DC

Built for South West Trains by Siemens between 2003 and 2006, this is the most numerous class of Desiro UK units. No. 450012 is seen tucked away in a quiet corner of the Watercress Line at Alresford (Hants) in April 2003 while static crew familiarisation tests were being undertaken.

Class 700/1 No. 700107, 25 kV 750 Volt DC

Built by Siemens for the Bedford–Brighton Thameslink service, the Class 700/1 trains entered service in July 2016. No. 700107 approaches Gatwick Airport station on a Bedford-bound working in September 2016.

Class 707 Desiro City No. 707005, 750 Volt DC

Ordered from Siemens by the successful Stagecoach South West Trains franchise in 2014, delivery commenced in 2017. However, despite operating the franchise successfully, Stagecoach controversially lost out to First South Western in the summer of 2017. The units have entered service with First South Western, operating from Waterloo to Windsor and Eton and Weybridge via Brentford. No. 707005 is seen at Clapham Junction not long after being delivered in July 2017.

Class 67 No. 67002, Bo-Bo, 3,200 hp

Built for English Welsh & Scottish Railway to work fast mail trains, but the mail contracts were lost by EWS in 2004. Since then the Class 67s have been employed by a variety of train-operating companies in a variety of activities. No. 67002 is captured doing what she was built for as she approaches the 1 in 37 Lickey Incline with the 1S81 Bristol–Shieldmuir mail train in June 2001.

Rail Freight Operators

Direct Rail Services (DRS)

Formed in 1994, initially to take over the movement of nuclear material using refurbished Class 20 locomotives, DRS is now part of the Nuclear Decommissioning Authority, and as such is the only publically owned railway operator in mainland UK.

Since 1997 it has diversified into intermodal traffic, principally between Daventry and Scotland. Locomotives are also hired out for some passenger services, predominantly in East Anglia and Cumbria. The locomotive fleet consists of Class 20s, 37s, 47s, and 66s, as well as new Class 68s and 88s.

Nos 20312 and 20313

Nos 20312 and 20313 are captured preparing to tackle the Lickey Incline with the 7M53 Bridgewater–Crewe nuclear flask service in August 2000.

Class 66/4 No. 66429

Class 66/4 No. 66429 powers the 4S47 Daventy–Coatbridge Malcolm freight working through Nuneaton in September 2012.

Class 68 No. 68008 *Avenger*, Bo-Bo, 3,800 hp

No. 68008 *Avenger* sports DRS livery as it brings the late-running Chiltern Trains Marylebone–Birmingham (Snow Hill)–Kidderminster service into Snow Hill in June 2015.

Class 88 No. 88003 *Genesis*, Electro-Diesel, 25 kV, 5,000 hp/Diesel, 710 hp

Introduced in 2017, the Class 88 locomotives combine 5,000 hp electric traction with an auxiliary diesel. These are the first electro-diesel locomotives with the combination of overhead electric transmission rather than third rail. No. 88003 *Genesis* is seen at Lambrigg (Cumberland) on a Mossend–Daventry working. (Dieseldude321, Flickr)

Freightliner

Freightliner was formed in 1995, taking over British Rail container operations originally established during the 1960s Beeching era. It also established a 'heavy haul' business in 1999.

It is now part of a highly successful international operation and is the second largest rail freight operator in the United Kingdom, serving major ports and inland freight terminals.

Initially operating a collection of elderly Class 47 diesel locomotives and Class 86 and 90 electric locomotives, Class 66 and 70 diesel locomotives were later acquired.

No. 47289

Built at Crewe in 1966, No. 47289 stills sports the original Freightliner two-tone grey with red flash livery when seen in April 2001. Even after thirty-five years, she is capable of racing the 4E74 Southampton–Leeds train past Didcot.

No. 66574

No. 66574 brings the 4E24 Thamesport–Leeds train into Doncaster in June 2009.

Class 86 No. 86613

The Class 86 units date from the 1960s, and No. 86613 was built at Doncaster in 1965. Modified for freight work in the late 1980s, it is seen 'dead in tow' while passing through Stratford on a northbound Freightliner working in 2016.

No. 90048

No. 90048 still sports the two-tone grey and red flash livery as she sets off south from Preston with the 4L60 Coatbridge–Ipswich train in July 2001.

Class 70 No. 70020, Co-Co, 3,690 hp

The Class 70s were built from 2009 to 2017 by General Electric at Erie (PA) for both heavy haul and container trains. Irrespective of safety considerations, they would not win any prizes for good looks. No. 70020 comes off the Felixstowe branch at Westerfield (Suffolk) with the 4M93 Felixstowe–Birmingham (Lawley Street) container service. It will run under the wires from Ipswich to Birmingham.

GB Railfreight

GB Railfreight became operational in April 2001. Unlike other operators, it does not owe its origins to a piece of the former British Rail freight operations; starting from an initial contract to operate infrastructure trains in 2001, it acquired its first intermodal container contract in 2002. It has grown successfully to have 15 per cent of the rail freight market with a fleet of 120 locomotives, serving a wide variety of customers.

A commendable sense of tradition pervades through the company, which has a particular association with the Great Central Railway.

No. 66707 *Sir Sam Fay*

GB Railfreight ordered its first Class 66 locomotives in 2000. No. 66707 *Sir Sam Fay* honours the famous Edwardian manager of the Great Central Railway, and the locomotive is seen on the former Great Central Railway passing Barnetby with the 6H33 Immingham–Drax train in June 2009.

Open Access Passenger Services

Hull Trains

An open access operator currently owned by FirstGroup, Hull Trains has a track access agreement to operate a six-trains-a-day service between London (King's Cross) and Hull/Beverley until 2029.

No. 222103

No. 222103 is seen leaving London King's Cross with the 16.12 service to Hull in July 2005.

Grand Central Trains

Another open access operator owned by Arriva, Grand Central Trains was established in 2007 to provide services to London King's Cross from Bradford and Wakefield (Kirkgate) – the West Yorkshire service – and Sunderland and Hartlepool – the North Eastern service. A combination of Class 43 HSTs and the Class 180 Adelente units is employed.

Class 180

Travelling too fast to catch the number, a Class 180 speeds past Alexandra Palace with the 16.03 King's Cross–Bradford service in October 2017.

Reopening and New Projects

After years of neglect, the last twenty years have seen a major railway renaissance. Since 1996 the number of passengers using the railways has doubled, while freight has increased by 70 per cent. This has led to new services, reopening of closed or mothballed lines, and new projects.

Crossrail (The Elizabeth Line)

One of the largest rail construction projects since the Channel Tunnel link, by 2019 this line will run from Heathrow Airport and Reading under Central London to Shenfield in Essex and Abbey Wood in South East London.

No. 345005

At the time of writing, the new Class 345 trains had started to appear on the Great Eastern section. No. 345005 approaches Chadwell Heath on a gloomy August morning in 2017.

The Great Western Electrification

Described when it was announced in 2009 as the biggest investment in the former Great Western Railway since Brunel built it, the project was to electrify the lines from London to Bristol, Oxford and South Wales along with the direct line from Reading to Taunton. The plan was for completion in 2019.

Reality intervened and in 2016 it was announced that the electrification from Didcot to Oxford, the direct route to Bristol via Bath and projects around Windsor and Heathrow were to be deferred indefinitely.

In March 2017 the Public Accounts Committee reported that the project was way over budget and the victim of chronic mismanagement.

In July 2017 it was announced that the electrification to Swansea had been cancelled. However, as of autumn 2017, the electrification as far as Maidenhead has been completed and is operational.

Class 387/1 No. 387138

Bombardier-built Class 387/1 EMU No. 387138 runs into Slough en route to Paddington in September 2017.

Class 800 No. 800005

The Hitachi-built Class 800 that will provide the inter-city services to Bristol and South Wales are bimodal – capable of running as 25 kV overhead electric units and as diesel-electric units. They entered service in October 2017, but were plagued with numerous technical faults. Delayed due to technical problems, No. 800005 forms the rear of the late-running 11.45 Paddington to South Wales service as it leaves Reading on 6 November 2017.

The Chiltern Line to Oxford

Historically, the London & North Western Railway operated cross-country lines from Oxford to Cambridge via Bletchley and Bedford. The line from Bedford was closed under Beeching, while the line south from Bletchley was largely mothballed with limited freight use. Enterprising Chiltern Railways installed a curve from the former Great Western line to Banbury and now operates a highly lucrative and successful service from Marylebone to Oxford.

Much of the success is derived from visitors to the Bicester Village Market, which is adjacent to the former London & North Western station.

Plans to reconnect/reopen the line from Bicester to Bletchley, as well as to connect Aylesbury with Bletchley and Milton Keynes, have been authorised.

No. 168110

No. 168110 arrives at Bicester Village from Marylebone on 7 September 2017. The entrance to the shopping village is on the opposite platform.